Perfect
PUDDINGS
& DESSERTS

GW00402311

Desserts are the icing on the cake, as the saying goes. They certainly make a meal seem special, no matter the occasion – tonight's family dinner or a special celebration. This compendium of sweet courses includes everyone's old-fashioned favourites as well as many exciting new ways to conclude the evening meal. They're all designed to make that last course the one the family most looks forward to.

Even with today's busy lifestyle there's no need to drop dessert from everyday meals when you've a number of easy, economical simply divine delights from which to choose. As Summer's bounty ripens, offer the family chilled jellies, moulds or baked treats filled with the heady fragrances and flavours of perfect fresh fruit – or choose a sorbet or ice cream . . . so sophisticated in flavour, but child's play to create.

At the first sign of cold weather, turn your thoughts – and these pages – to warm soul-satisfying steamed puddings, hot pies, cobblers and custards to raise the family's spirits on chilly nights.

And when it's time for a dinner party dazzler, look through our irresistible temptations to delight your guests for, whatever your preference – sweet and spicy, fruit-filled, frozen or flambéed, you're sure to find the perfect finale.

CONTENTS

EASY ECONOMICAL STANDBYS

From baked nursery favourites to light-as-air whips and parfaits, this selection of quick and easy desserts will satisfy both tastebuds and budget.

Steamed Canary Puddings

125g (4oz) butter
1 tspn finely grated lemon rind
170g (5¹/₂oz) caster sugar
2 eggs
185g (6oz) self-raising flour
60-125ml (2-4fl oz) milk

1 Beat butter and lemon rind until creamy, then slowly beat in sugar until light and fluffy. Add eggs, one at a time, with a tablespoon of the measured flour. Beat well then fold in remaining flour alternately with enough milk to make a dough of dropping consistency.

2 Spoon mixture into six greased dariole moulds, loosely cover with foil or buttered greaseproof paper and tie securely. Stand moulds on a rack in a saucepan filled with enough boiling water to come halfway up sides of moulds. Cover pan and steam for 30-35 minutes or until cooked.

3 Turn onto heated serving dishes and serve hot with custard, cream or sweet sauce.

Serves 6

Kitchen Tip
For a single pudding, three-quarter fill a greased 1.2-1.5 litre (2-2¹/₂pt) pudding basin with mixture, cover with lid or double thickness of greaseproof paper, with a pleat across the middle to allow for expansion. Tie with string and steam for 1¹/₂-2 hours.

Variations
Waterfall Pudding: Place 2 tablespoons jam, marmalade or golden syrup in bottom of each mould before adding pudding mixture.

Fruit Pudding: Add 155g (5oz) mixed dried fruit with the flour and a little more milk to make a soft dropping consistency.

Orange Pudding: Cream 2 teaspoons grated orange rind with the butter, add 1 tablespoon orange marmalade and 60ml (2fl oz) orange juice instead of milk.

Chocolate Pudding: Sift 2 tablespoons cocoa powder with the flour and cream 1 tablespoon jam, honey or syrup with the butter.

Spiced Raisin Pudding: Sift 1 teaspoon mixed spice with the flour and add 125g (4oz) chopped raisins with the flour. Use a little more milk if necessary.

Marmalade Cream Sauce

2 tblspn orange marmalade
125ml (4fl oz) double cream
1 tblspn brandy

Combine marmalade and cream in a small saucepan and stir constantly over low heat until marmalade melts. Do not allow the sauce to boil. Stir in brandy and serve.

Serves 4-6

Steamed Canary Puddings, Pineapple Mists (page 5), with Almond Bread (page 46); Pears Hélène, Apricots Cardinal (page 4)

Pears Hélène

500ml (16fl oz) vanilla ice cream

440g (14oz) canned pear halves, drained

toasted flaked almonds

Hot Chocolate Sauce

185ml (6fl oz) water

125g (4oz) sugar

60g (2oz) dark chocolate, chopped

single cream, sherry or brandy for thinning

1 To make sauce, combine water and sugar in a saucepan and simmer, stirring until sugar dissolves. Simmer for 5 minutes or until syrupy. Add chocolate and stir to combine. If too thick, add cream, sherry or brandy to thin. Serve immediately or keep warm in a double saucepan or bowl over warm water.

2 Scoop ice cream into dessert dishes. Place two pear halves on top with chocolate sauce. Sprinkle with almonds.

Serves 4

Puffed Banana Fritters

60g (2oz) caster sugar

1¹/₂ tspn ground cinnamon or cardamom

250g (8oz) plain flour

2 tspn baking powder

1 tspn salt

2 tspn unsalted butter

250g (8oz) mashed ripe bananas

vegetable oil for frying

1 Combine sugar and spice. In another bowl, sift together flour, baking powder and salt. Rub in butter with fingertips until mixture resembles breadcrumbs. Stir in bananas and 6 tablespoons water or enough to make a soft, not sticky dough.

2 Knead dough on a lightly floured surface until smooth. Roll out thinly and cut into 5cm (2in) squares. Cover squares with a damp tea-towel.

3 Heat oil in a large saucepan until a cube of bread dropped in browns in 50 seconds and fry pastries, in batches, until puffed and golden. Drain on paper towels and sprinkle immediately with spiced sugar. Keep warm in a preheated 125°C (250°F/Gas ¹/₂) oven.

Makes 12-18 fritters

Apricots Cardinal

440g (14oz) canned apricot halves, drained

500ml (16fl oz) vanilla ice cream

¹/₂ x quantity Raspberry Sauce (recipe page 38)

Arrange apricots with scoops of ice cream in four dessert dishes, spoon sauce over and serve.

Serves 4

Puffed Banana Fritters

Plum Meringue Pudding

Plum Meringue Pudding

90g (3oz) sugar

2 tspn finely grated orange rind

3-4 tblspn fresh orange juice

60ml (2fl oz) water

750g (1¹/₂lb) fresh plums, halved and stoned

185g (6oz) day-old crustless bread, cubed

60g (2oz) butter

2 egg yolks

1 tspn ground cinnamon

Meringue

2 egg whites

75g (2¹/₂oz) caster sugar

1 Place sugar, orange rind, orange juice and water in a medium saucepan and bring to simmering, stirring until sugar dissolves and mixture forms a syrup. Add plums and gently poach until just tender. Remove from heat. Place bread cubes in a bowl. Pour syrup from plums over bread and let soak a few minutes.

2 Preheat oven to 180°C (350°F/ Gas 4). Cream butter until light, beat in egg yolks until creamy, then beat in soaked bread and cinnamon. Fold in plums and turn into a buttered soufflé dish. Bake for 30 minutes.

3 To make meringue, beat egg whites until stiff, fold in sugar and spoon over pudding, swirling decoratively. Return to oven, reduce heat to 150°C (300°F/ Gas 2) and bake for 10 minutes longer or until meringue is set and golden.

Serves 6

Pineapple Mists

3¹/₂ tspn gelatine

125ml (4fl oz) water

60g (2oz) sugar

185ml (6fl oz) pineapple juice

1 tblspn fresh lemon juice

2 egg whites, stiffly beaten

1 Soften gelatine in water, then stir over simmering water until dissolved. Add sugar, stirring until dissolved. Stir in pineapple and lemon juices.

2 Chill mixture until slightly thickened, then beat with an electric mixer, adding beaten egg whites, until mixture is quite thick. Spoon into a serving bowl or six individual dishes. Decorate with chopped fresh fruit and serve with sweet biscuits.

Serves 6

Lemon Parfaits

Lemon Parfaits

1 tblspn finely grated lemon rind

125ml (4fl oz) fresh lemon juice

3 large eggs, separated

170g (5^1/$_2$oz) sugar

250ml (8fl oz) double cream, stiffly whipped

lemon rind slivers and sugared violets to decorate, optional

1 In a small, enamelled saucepan, combine lemon rind, lemon juice, egg yolks and half the sugar. Beat well then stir over low heat, without boiling, until thick. Cool.

2 Beat egg whites to soft peaks, beat in remaining sugar until they hold stiff peaks and fold into lemon mixture with whipped cream. Turn mixture into stemmed glasses and chill.

Serves 6

Nougat Crumble Pie

60g (2oz) butter

60g (2oz) caster sugar

1 egg yolk

1 tblspn milk

60g (2oz) self-raising flour

60g (2oz) plain flour

pinch salt

Nougat Filling

60g (2oz) crumbled plain cake or breadcrumbs, made from stale bread

60g (2oz) sugar

90g (3oz) desiccated coconut

30g (1oz) finely chopped nuts

2 tspn finely grated lemon rind

2 tblspn fresh lemon juice

1 tblspn apricot jam

1 egg white, stiffly beaten

1 tspn ground cinnamon mixed with 1 tspn brown sugar

1 Cream together butter and sugar then stir in egg yolk and milk. Gradually add combined sifted flours and salt, mixing to a firm dough. Wrap and chill for 30 minutes. Roll out pastry and line an 18-20cm (7-8in) pie plate or flan tin with removable base.

2 Preheat oven to 200°C (400°F/ Gas 6). To make filling, combine crumbs, sugar, coconut, nuts, lemon rind, lemon juice and jam. Fold in egg white. Turn mixture into pastry case, sprinkle with cinnamon-sugar mixture and bake for 10 minutes.

3 Reduce heat to 180°C (350°F/ Gas 4) and continue baking for 10 minutes longer or until filling is golden. Serve warm or cold with cream or ice cream.

Serves 6

Sour Cream Cheesecake

125g (4oz) plain sweet biscuits, crushed

6 tblspn ground almonds

60ml (2fl oz) double cream

90g (3oz) butter, melted

Cheese Filling

500g (1lb) cream cheese, softened

125g (4oz) sugar

2 eggs

1 tspn finely grated lemon rind

1 tspn fresh lemon juice

1¹/₂ tspn vanilla essence

¹/₂ tspn grated nutmeg

Cream Topping

375g (12oz) sour cream

2 tblspn sugar

¹/₂ tspn vanilla esssence

¹/₂ tspn grated nutmeg

1 Stir together biscuit crumbs, almonds, cream and melted butter and press mixture into a 23cm (9in) springform tin to come 5cm (2in) up the sides. Chill.

2 Preheat oven to 190°C (375°F/ Gas 5). To make filling, beat together cream cheese and sugar until smooth, then beat in eggs, one at a time, adding lemon rind, lemon juice and vanilla essence.

Pour mixture into chilled crust and bake for 20 minutes. Remove from oven, dust with nutmeg and set aside to cool to room temperature.

3 Increase oven temperature to 220°C (425°F/Gas 7). To make topping, beat together sour cream, sugar and vanilla essence until smooth and pour over cheesecake. Bake for 5 minutes or until topping is just melted. Cool cake to room temperature, cover and chill for 6-12 hours. Dust with nutmeg before serving.

Serves 8-10

Sour Cream Cheesecake

Baked Caramel Pears

6 firm-ripe pears, peeled and halved

60g (2oz) butter, melted

2 tblspn plain flour

1 tspn vanilla essence

90g (3oz) brown sugar

1/2 tspn ground cinnamon

90ml (3fl oz) double cream

90g (3oz) sour cream

1 Preheat oven to 160°C (325°F/ Gas 3). Scoop out core from pears, score round side of pears at 5mm (1/4in) intervals and arrange, cut side down, in a buttered ovenproof dish.

2 Combine remaining ingredients except cream and sour cream and spread mixture over pears. Bake for 10 minutes, reduce heat to 180°C (350°F/Gas 4) and bake for 15-20 minutes longer or until pears are tender.

3 Beat cream until slightly thickened, stir in sour cream and serve with warm pears.

Serves 6

Treacle Sponge Pudding

2 tblspn golden syrup

2 tblspn fresh lemon juice

1 tblspn dried breadcrumbs

125g (4oz) butter

1 tspn finely grated lemon rind

100g (3¹/₂oz) caster sugar

2 large eggs

155g (5oz) self-raising flour, sifted

pinch salt

milk

1 Butter a 1.2-1.5 litre (2-2¹/₂pt) pudding basin. Combine golden syrup, lemon juice and breadcrumbs in the basin. In a mixing bowl, cream butter with lemon rind, gradually adding sugar until light and fluffy. Beat in eggs, one at a time. Fold in flour and salt, alternately, with enough milk to make a dropping consistency.

2 Turn mixture into prepared basin, top with a round of greaseproof paper and cover with foil, securing with string. Place basin on a rack or upturned saucer in a large saucepan quarter-filled with boiling water. Cover pan with lid and steam for 1¹/₂ hours, adding more water if necessary during cooking.

3 Turn pudding out and serve, if liked, with more golden syrup warmed with a little lemon juice to sharpen the taste.

Serves 6

Baked Rice Cream

500ml (16fl oz) milk

125ml (4fl oz) double cream

2 tblspn short-grain rice, washed

2 eggs

1 egg yolk

60g (2oz) caster sugar

pinch salt

1/2 tspn vanilla essence

freshly grated nutmeg

1 Bring milk and cream to simmering in a heavy saucepan, add rice and simmer, stirring, for 20 minutes. Remove from heat.

2 Preheat oven to 160°C (325°F/ Gas 3). Gently stir together eggs, egg yolk, sugar, salt and vanilla essence. Pour about one-third of the rice mixture into egg mixture, stirring constantly, then return mixture to saucepan and stir until sugar dissolves. Pour mixture into a 1.2 litre (2pt) ovenproof dish.

3 Place dish in a baking tin filled with enough hot water to come halfway up the sides of the dish. Stir custard to distribute rice, sprinkle with nutmeg and bake for 30-40 minutes or until a knife inserted near centre comes out clean.

4 Serve hot with stewed fruit, sliced banana or one of the sauce variations.

Serves 6

Variations

Strawberry Sauce: Purée 250g (8oz) fresh or frozen strawberries (or raspberries). Stir in 1-2 tablespoons caster sugar, cover and chill for 1-2 hours. The berries will produce syrup as they stand. Stir again before serving.

Apricot Sauce: Drain 220g (7oz) canned apricot halves, reserving syrup and purée fruit until smooth. Place purée in a saucepan with 125ml (4fl oz) reserved syrup, 60g (2oz) sugar and 2 teaspoons cornflour mixed with 60ml (2fl oz) sherry. Heat, stirring, until sauce boils and thickens. Remove from heat and stir in 2 teaspoons grated lemon rind. Serve hot or cool.

Caramel Sauce: Melt 1 tablespoon butter with 170g (5¹/₂oz) brown sugar in a small, heavy saucepan. Bring to the boil and boil for 30 seconds. Remove from heat and stir in 220ml (7fl oz) canned reduced cream.

Coffee Pecan Marshmallow

12 marshmallows

1 tspn instant coffee powder

60ml (2fl oz) boiling water

60ml (2fl oz) dark rum

250ml (8fl oz) double cream

60g (2oz) chopped pecans

1 With scissors, snip marsh-mallows into quarters and place in a bowl. Dissolve coffee in boiling water, add rum, pour mixture over marshmallows and stir briskly. Allow to cool, stirring occasionally.

2 Beat cream to soft peaks and fold in marshmallow mixture and nuts, reserving 3 teaspoons nuts. Spoon mixture into individual dishes, garnish with reserved nuts and chill until served.

Serves 4

Baked Caramel Pears

FROZEN FANTASIES

For a refreshing finale there's nothing quite like a palate cleansing sorbet or flavoured ice cream. Children – of all ages – just love them!

Tangy Lemon Ice

500ml (16fl oz) water

315g (10oz) sugar

500ml (16fl oz) strained fresh lemon juice

1 Combine water and sugar in a heavy saucepan and bring to the boil, stirring until sugar dissolves. Then simmer for 1-2 minutes or until a syrup forms. Remove from heat, stir in lemon juice and set aside to cool completely.

2 Pour mixture into a freezer container and freeze, beating occasionally with an electric mixer or whisk, until solid, or use an ice cream maker.

Makes about 1 litre (1³/₄pt)

Apricot Macaroon Ice Cream

300g (9¹/₂oz) dried apricots

1 tblspn lemon juice

375ml (12fl oz) double cream

185ml (6fl oz) milk

4 large egg yolks

125g (4oz) caster sugar

90g (3oz) crisp almond macaroons, coarsely crushed

orange-flavoured liqueur

1 Soak apricots overnight in just enough water to cover. Transfer undrained apricots to a saucepan and cook over a low heat until soft. Remove from heat, add lemon juice and set aside to cool slightly. Place mixture in a food processor or blender and purée until smooth. Chill.

2 Heat cream and milk until scalded. Beat egg yolks with sugar until thick and pale, slowly stir in hot milk mixture. Return mixture to saucepan and cook over a low heat, stirring constantly, until slightly thickened. Cool, then chill thoroughly.

3 Combine purée and custard and pour into a freezer container. Freeze, stirring occasionally, until almost solid, fold in macaroons and return to freezer until solid, or use an ice cream maker. Serve with a splash of liqueur.

Makes about 1 litre (1³/₄pt)

Melon and Mint Sorbet

4 tblspn sugar

60ml (2fl oz) water

1/2 bunch fresh mint

1 very ripe cantaloupe or rockmelon

mint leaves or thin melon slices to decorate

1 Combine sugar and water in a saucepan, bring to the boil, stirring until sugar dissolves, and boil for 1 minute. Add mint leaves, remove from heat and set aside to cool.

2 Halve melon, scoop out seeds, then scoop flesh into a blender or food processor. Add mint syrup and purée until smooth.

3 Pour mixture into a freezer container and freeze, beating with an electric mixer or processing mixture several times, until solid, or use an ice cream maker.

4 For easier scooping, place sorbet in the refrigerator for 30 minutes before serving. Decorate with fresh mint or melon.

Makes about 600mL (1pt)

Tangy Lemon Ice, Apricot Macaroon Ice Cream, Melon and Mint Sorbet, Coffee Granita (page 12)

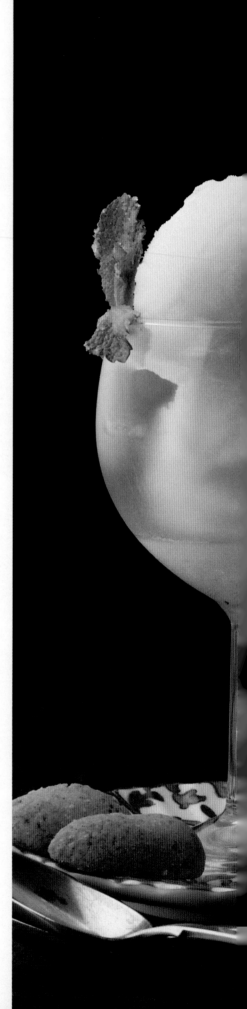

Coconut Ice Cream

375ml (12fl oz) double cream

375ml (12fl oz) milk

90g (3oz) desiccated coconut

2 eggs

2 egg yolks

125g (4oz) sugar

pinch salt

toasted shredded coconut for serving

1 Combine cream, milk and coconut in a saucepan and heat over a very low heat, without boiling, for 15 minutes. Cover and cool to room temperature. Blend mixture briefly in a food processor then strain through a sieve, rubbing to extract as much liquid as possible from the coconut. Discard coconut pulp.

2 Beat eggs, egg yolks, sugar and salt in a heatproof bowl until thick. Place over simmering water, add coconut liquid and cook, stirring, until slightly thickened. Remove from heat, place over a pan of iced water and allow to cool, stirring occasionally.

3 Pour mixture into a freezer container, cover and freeze until firm. Scoop into bowls and decorate with lightly toasted shredded coconut.

Makes about 1 litre (1³/4pt)

Honey Ice Cream

4 eggs

2 egg yolks

1 litre (1³/4pt) double cream

260g (8¹/2oz) honey

Beat together eggs and egg yolks until thick and pale. Stir in cream and honey. Pour into a freezer container and freeze, stirring or whisking occasionally, until solid, or use an ice cream maker.

Makes about 1.2 litres (2pt)

Coffee Granita

500ml (16fl oz) hot strong black coffee

sugar to taste

freshly whipped double cream, sweetened to taste

1 While the coffee is still piping hot, stir in sugar until dissolved. Cool completely, then chill thoroughly.

2 Pour mixture into a freezer container and freeze, beating with an electric mixer or processing mixture several times, until solid, or use an ice cream maker.

3 For easier serving, break up granita, place in a food processor and process to a fine-textured soft ice. Spoon into chilled goblets and garnish with cream.

Makes about 600mL (1pt)

Coconut Ice Cream

Cinnamon Ice Cream

Cinnamon Ice Cream

Serve with hot peaches either poached or gently fried in a little butter with sugar.

315ml (10fl oz) milk

200ml (6¹/₂fl oz) double cream

1 stick cinnamon

1 tblspn freshly ground cinnamon

125g (4oz) sugar

200ml (6¹/₂fl oz) water

6 egg yolks

1 Combine milk, cream, cinnamon stick and ground cinnamon in a heavy saucepan and heat over a very low heat, without boiling, for 15 minutes. Cover and cool to room temperature. Discard cinnamon stick.

2 Dissolve sugar in water over low heat, bring to the boil and boil rapidly until syrup reaches 120°C (250°F) when tested with a sugar thermometer, or until a little syrup dropped into cold water will form a hard ball.

3 Beat egg yolks until thick and creamy then gradually add boiling syrup in a thin, steady stream, beating constantly until mixture is cold, thick and fluffy. Add cinnamon liquid and mix well.

4 Pour mixture into a freezer container and freeze, stirring or whisking mixture several times, until solid, or use an ice cream maker.

Makes about 1 litre (1³/₄pt)

Italian Coffee Ice Cream

500ml (16fl oz) double cream

185g (6oz) fresh coffee beans

6 egg yolks

100g (3¹/₂oz) caster sugar

1 Combine cream and coffee beans in a saucepan and heat until scalded. Beat egg yolks and sugar until light and pale, gradually add hot cream with beans and mix well. Return mixture to saucepan and cook over a low heat, stirring, until custard slightly thickens. Cool to room temperature.

2 Strain mixture into a freezer container, cover and freeze, without stirring, until firm. Serve with strawberries or a crisp dessert biscuit (recipes page 46).

Makes about 600ml (1pt)

Espresso and Ice Cream

This is not a dessert for your finest crystal or delicate glasses. Sturdy yet attractive goblets will do the job admirably.

8-12 small scoops vanilla ice cream

12 tblspn very hot espresso coffee

crisp dessert biscuits to serve

Place 2-3 scoops of ice cream into each of four dessert glasses. Pour 3 tablespoons espresso over each and serve immediately with dessert biscuits (recipes page 46).

Serves 4

Fresh Peach Ice Cream

625g (20oz) ripe peaches, peeled and stoned

315g (10oz) caster sugar

500ml (16fl oz) double cream, very softly whipped

250ml (8fl oz) milk

1 tspn vanilla essence

1 Purée peaches with sugar in a food processor or blender.

2 Place purée, cream, milk and vanilla essence in a freezer container, mix well and freeze, stirring mixture once or twice until solid, or use an ice cream maker. Keep well covered and use within 2 days.

Makes about 1 litre (1³/4pt)

Buttermilk Sorbet

500ml (16fl oz) buttermilk

90g (3oz) sugar

440g (14oz) canned crushed pineapple, drained

1 egg white

1 tspn vanilla essence

Combine buttermilk, sugar and pineapple in a freezer container and freeze until mushy. Place in a chilled bowl, add egg white and vanilla and beat until fluffy. Return to container, cover and freeze until firm, stirring occasionally.

Makes about 600ml (1pt)

Fresh Strawberry Sorbet

1kg (2lb) ripe strawberries, hulled and puréed

90ml (3fl oz) fresh orange juice

2 tblspn fresh lemon juice

440g (14oz) sugar

125ml (4fl oz) water

2 egg whites

1 Combine strawberry purée, orange juice and lemon juice and chill thoroughly.

2 Stir sugar and water in a saucepan over low heat until sugar dissolves, bring to the boil and boil for 2 minutes. Cool and chill thoroughly.

3 Combine fruit and syrup in a freezer container and freeze until mushy. Turn into a chilled bowl and beat well until light and thick. Beat egg whites to a stiff foam and fold into sorbet. Return to container and freeze until firm.

4 Transfer sorbet to a mould or serving bowl, cover and freeze for 2 hours longer before serving. Sorbet will keep for 1-2 days, but is really at its best if eaten within 6 hours.

Makes about 1 litre (1³/4pt)

Kitchen Tip
To prepare this sorbet in an ice cream maker, omit the egg whites. Combine berry purée and syrup in container of machine and process as directed.

Watermelon Ice

750g (1lb 8oz) seeded and diced watermelon

125g (4oz) sugar

2-3 tblspn strained fresh lemon juice

fresh mint leaves to decorate

Place watermelon in a blender and blend at medium speed for 30 seconds, or push through a coarse sieve. Combine purée, sugar and lemon juice and mix well. Pour mixture into a freezer container and freeze until firm. Transfer sorbet to a chilled bowl and beat until smooth. Return to freezer container, cover and freeze until firm. Spoon into glass serving dishes and decorate with mint.

Makes about 750ml (1¹/4pt)

Kitchen Tip
This makes a great summer party sweet. Pile it up into clear glass dishes and decorate each with a fresh sprig of mint. It is best eaten when just made to capture the fresh taste.

Frozen Peach Mousse

This is best eaten the day it is made.

3 large ripe peaches, peeled and stoned

170g (5¹/2oz) caster sugar

250ml (8fl oz) double cream, whipped

Strawberry Coulis

250g (8oz) ripe strawberries, crushed

2 tblspn caster sugar

1 Lightly mash peach flesh with sugar and fold into whipped cream. Turn mixture into a freezer container, cover and freeze, without stirring, until firm.

2 To make coulis, crush strawberries with sugar and chill, stirring occasionally, until sugar dissolves. Serve over scoops of mousse.

Serves 6

OLD-FASHIONED FAVOURITES

From winter warmers to family puddings this selection of classic favourites is sure to delight dessert lovers.

Queen of Puddings

This is a marvellous old-fashioned recipe. Make it with raspberry, plum or apricot jam or ginger marmalade.

500ml (16fl oz) milk, scalded

3 eggs, separated

1 tspn vanilla essence

1 tblspn sugar

6 slices white bread, crusts removed and cubed

2 tblspn caster sugar

3 tblspn raspberry jam

1 Preheat oven to 180°C (350°F/ Gas 4). Combine hot milk, egg yolks, vanilla essence and 1 tablespoon sugar and beat until combined. Stir in bread cubes. Pour mixture into a lightly greased ovenproof dish. Place dish in a baking tin filled with enough hot water to come halfway up sides of dish and bake for 45 minutes.

2 Beat egg whites until stiff, then fold in caster sugar. Spread jam over pudding and top with meringue. If liked, decorate meringue by dropping small teaspoons of extra jam on top.

3 Return to oven and bake for 15 minutes longer or until meringue is golden and crisp. Serve warm or at room temperature.

Serves 6

Golden Syrup Dumplings

250g (8oz) self-raising flour

pinch salt

45g (1¹/₂oz) butter

2 eggs, lightly beaten

a little milk

Syrup

500ml (16fl oz) water

90g (3oz) sugar

2 tblspn golden syrup

30g (1oz) butter

1 Sift together flour and salt and rub in butter with fingertips until mixture resembles coarse breadcrumbs. Using a knife, stir in eggs, adding enough milk to make a soft dough. Divide into 12 pieces and roll into balls.

2 To make syrup, heat water, sugar and golden syrup in a large saucepan, stirring until sugar dissolves. Add butter and bring to the boil. Add dumplings to syrup, cover and simmer, without lifting the lid, for 20 minutes.

3 Serve dumplings at once, with a little syrup spooned over them and accompanied with custard or pouring cream.

Serves 6

Queen of Puddings

Caramel Date Pudding

Orange Crisps

8 slices day-old white bread

185g (6oz) sugar

6 tblspn orange juice

60g (2oz) butter

1 tspn grated orange rind

ice cream for serving

1 Remove crusts from bread and cut each in two triangles. Combine sugar, orange juice and butter in a small saucepan and cook over low heat, stirring, for 5 minutes. Add orange rind.

2 Dip bread in syrup and place in a single layer on a lightly greased baking sheet. Cook under a preheated medium griller until brown on both sides. Serve at once with ice cream.

Serves 6

Caramel Date Pudding

250g (8oz) pitted dates

1 tspn grated fresh ginger or $^{1}/_{2}$ tspn ground ginger

315ml (10fl oz) water

1 tspn bicarbonate of soda

125g (4oz) unsalted butter

220g (7oz) caster sugar

$^{1}/_{2}$ tspn vanilla essence

3 large eggs

250g (8oz) self-raising flour

1 tspn ground ginger

Caramel Sauce

125g (4oz) unsalted butter

170g (5$^{1}/_{2}$oz) brown sugar

315ml (10fl oz) double cream

1 Place dates, ginger and water in a saucepan and bring slowly to the boil. Stir in bicarbonate of soda and cool.

2 Preheat oven to 180°C (350°F/ Gas 4). Cream butter, gradually adding sugar, until light and fluffy. Add vanilla essence and eggs, one at a time, beating well after each addition. Sift flour with ground ginger and fold into creamed mixture. Fold in date mixture.

3 Turn batter into a greased and paper-lined charlotte mould or 23cm (9in) round cake tin. Bake for 50 minutes or until risen, golden and cooked when tested with a skewer. If pudding browns too quickly, cover with a double sheet of brown paper.

4 To make sauce, combine butter, sugar and cream in a heavy saucepan and bring to the boil, stirring to dissolve sugar. Boil for 5 minutes, remove from heat and serve warm with pudding.

Serves 8

Apricot Nut Upside Down Cake

1 egg, separated

100g (3¹/₂oz) caster sugar

125ml (4fl oz) milk

30g (1oz) butter, melted

125g (4oz) self-raising flour sifted with ¹/₂ tspn salt

Topping and Glaze

75g (2¹/₂oz) butter

60g (2oz) brown sugar

8 dried apricots, soaked and drained

8 dessert prunes, stoned

6 walnut halves

1 Preheat oven to 190°C (375°F/ Gas 5). To make topping, cream butter with brown sugar and spread over bottom and sides of a greased and paper-lined 20cm (8in) round cake tin. Arrange apricots, prunes and walnuts in a pattern over creamed mixture.

2 Beat egg white stiffly, add egg yolk then gradually beat in sugar until light and fluffy. Add milk and butter, then lightly fold in flour mixture.

3 Spoon mixture into prepared tin. Bake for 20-25 minutes or until cake is cooked. Immediately invert onto a serving plate, let stand for a few minutes then lift off the tin. Serve warm with cream, ice cream or custard.

Serves 6-8

Pear Cobbler

6-8 ripe pears, peeled, cored and sliced

75g (2¹/₂oz) caster sugar

1 tblspn grated fresh ginger

1 tspn finely grated lemon rind

2 tblspn fresh lemon juice

185g (6oz) plain flour

1 tblspn baking powder

3 tblspn sugar, extra

90g (3oz) butter

1 egg, lightly beaten

90-125ml (3-4fl oz) milk

1 Preheat oven to 220°C (425°F/ Gas 7). In a large deep pie dish, toss pears with caster sugar, ginger, lemon rind and lemon juice.

2 Sift together flour, baking powder and 1 tablespoon of extra sugar. Rub in butter with fingertips until mixture resembles breadcrumbs. Combine egg with 90ml (3fl oz) milk and stir into flour mixture, adding remaining milk if needed, to make a soft, but not sticky, dough.

3 Knead dough lightly until smooth. With floured hands break off portions of dough and place over pears, pressing slightly to flatten. Brush tops with water or extra milk and sprinkle with remaining extra sugar.

4 Bake for 40 minutes or until topping is browned and pear syrup starts to bubble.

Serves 6

Pear Cobbler

Bread and Butter Pudding

90g (3oz) sultanas

2 tblspn almond or orange-flavoured liqueur

315ml (10fl oz) milk

60g (2oz) caster sugar

1 vanilla pod or 1 tspn vanilla essence

3 eggs

170ml (5¹/₂fl oz) double cream

butter

8 thin slices white bread

4 tblspn apricot jam

toasted flaked almonds

icing sugar for dusting

1 Soak sultanas in liqueur, covered, preferably overnight.

2 Heat milk, sugar and vanilla pod, if using, over very low heat for 10 minutes, cover and cool. Remove vanilla pod. If using vanilla essence, add to milk now. Beat eggs with cream, stir in milk mixture and set aside.

3 Butter bread and spread with half the jam. Make into sandwiches, trim off crusts and cut each diagonally into quarters. Arrange sandwiches in a buttered 1 litre (1³/₄pt) ovenproof dish and sprinkle with soaked sultanas. Pour egg mixture over and let soak for 30 minutes.

4 Preheat oven to 160°C (325°F/ Gas 3). Place dish in a baking tin filled with enough hot water to come halfway up the side of the dish. Bake for 50 minutes or until top is crisp and golden.

5 Heat remaining jam, adding a little hot water if necessary. Brush over pudding and sprinkle with almonds. Serve warm, dusted with icing sugar.

Serves 6

Apple Charlotte

This is one of the nicest things one can do with apples. It is most important to cook the apple purée until it is almost of jam-like consistency. A charlotte mould has deep sloping sides with two lugs on each side for easier handling.

1.5kg (3lb) apples, Golden Delicious are best

strip of lemon rind

brown sugar or apricot jam

white sandwich bread, crusts removed

90g (3oz) butter, melted

1 Core unpeeled apples and slice thickly. Place in a heavy saucepan with a nut of butter and lemon rind, cover tightly and cook gently until very soft. Rub apples through a coarse sieve and return to pan with brown sugar or apricot jam to sweeten to taste.

Apple Charlotte

Vanilla, Coffee and Chocolate Custard Pots with Cigarettes Russes (page 46)

2 Bring to the boil and boil, stirring, for 15 minutes or until mixture drops heavily from the spoon and leaves the sides of the pan.

3 Preheat oven to 190°C (375°F/ Gas 5). Remove crusts from bread and cut slices into long strips about 4cm (1¼in) wide. Dip strips into melted butter and arrange, overlapping, in base and around the sides of a charlotte mould. Fill with apple purée and top with remaining bread.

4 Bake for 40 minutes or until bread is crisp and golden. Unmould onto a serving dish and serve with a softly whipped cream or a sauce made by melting apricot jam with a little water and sherry.

Serves 6

Vanilla Custard Pots

250ml (8fl oz) double cream
375ml (12fl oz) milk
1 vanilla pod or 1 tspn vanilla essence
1 tblspn caster sugar
1 egg
4 egg yolks

1 Heat cream, milk, vanilla pod, if using, and sugar over very low heat, without boiling, for 10 minutes, cover and cool slightly. Remove vanilla pod. If using vanilla essence, add to milk now.

2 Preheat oven to 150°C (300°F/ Gas 2). Beat egg and egg yolks lightly, stir in cream mixture then strain into a jug. Pour custard carefully into small ceramic pots or soufflé cups. Place in a shallow baking tin filled with enough hot water to come three-quarters up the sides of the pots. Cover pots with lids or foil and bake for 20-40 minutes or until set.

3 Turn off oven and allow pots to cool in oven for 30 minutes. Remove pots from tin, remove lids quickly and cool completely. Replace clean lids and chill until ready to serve.

Serves 6

Variations
Coffee Custard Pots: Omit vanilla pod. Add 125g (4oz) lightly crushed coffee beans and 60g (2oz) caster sugar to the cream and milk and slowly bring to scalding point. Continue from Step 2.
Chocolate Custard Pots: Add 2 tablespoons caster sugar and 125g (4oz) dark chocolate to the cream and milk and slowly bring to scalding point. Continue from Step 2.

Apple Pie Classic

250g (8oz) plain flour

pinch salt

1/2 tspn baking powder

185g (6oz) butter

1 egg yolk

1 tblspn sugar

1 tblspn cold water

Apple Filling

6-7 cooking apples

185g (6oz) sugar

1 tblspn plain flour

1 tspn ground cinnamon

pinch ground nutmeg

pinch salt

30g (1oz) butter

1 egg white, slightly beaten

extra sugar

whipped double cream, for serving

1 Sift together flour, salt and baking powder and rub in butter with fingertips until mixture resembles fine breadcrumbs. Add egg yolk, sugar and water to flour mixture and mix to make a dough. Do not knead. Shape dough into a ball, wrap and chill for 1 hour.

2 Preheat oven to 200°C (400°F/ Gas 6). Reserve one-third of the pastry. Roll out remainder on a lightly floured surface to line a greased 23cm (9in) pie plate.

3 To make filling, peel, core and slice apples. Combine sugar, flour, spices and salt and toss with apple slices. Spoon mixture into pastry case and dot with butter. Roll out remaining pastry to cover pie. Trim edges, pressing together in flutes. Brush with egg white to glaze, make steam vents and sprinkle lightly with extra sugar.

4 Bake for 1-1 1/4 hours or until pastry is golden and filling bubbly. Reduce heat if pastry browns too quickly. Serve warm with whipped cream.

Serves 6

Strawberry Rhubarb Cobbler

1kg (2lb) rhubarb, trimmed

250g (8oz) sugar

2 tblspn cornflour

90ml (3fl oz) water

500g (1lb) strawberries, hulled and halved

1 tspn finely grated orange rind

185g (6oz) plain flour

pinch salt

1 tblspn baking powder

60g (2oz) butter

1 egg, lightly beaten

60ml (2fl oz) milk

1 Preheat oven to 200°C (400°F/ Gas 6). Cut rhubarb into 3cm (1 1/4in) pieces and toss with combined sugar and cornflour in a buttered 1.5 litre (2 1/2pt) baking dish. Pour water over mixture.

2 Cover and bake for 20-30 minutes or until rhubarb is tender. Mix in strawberries and sprinkle with orange rind.

3 Sift together flour, salt and baking powder and rub in butter with fingertips until mixture resembles fine breadcrumbs. Add combined egg and milk and mix to make a dough of dropping consistency.

4 Drop large spoonfuls of dough over fruit and sprinkle with extra sugar. Bake for 15-20 minutes or until topping is golden.

Serves 6-8

Carrot Pudding

30g (1oz) butter

185g (6oz) self-raising flour

90g (3oz) brown sugar

1/4 tspn grated nutmeg

155g (5oz) mixed dried fruit

125g (4oz) carrots, grated

1 egg, beaten

3 tblspn milk

1 Rub butter into flour until mixture resembles bread-crumbs. Stir in sugar, nutmeg, fruit and carrots. Add combined egg and milk and mix to combine.

2 Spoon mixture into a greased 1.2-1.5 litre (2-2 1/2pt) pudding basin, cover with foil and tie securely. Place on a rack in a saucepan filled with enough hot water to come halfway up the sides of the basin, cover and steam for 1 1/2 hours.

Serves 6

Date and Apple Crisp

250g (8oz) dates, pitted

125ml (4fl oz) water

1 tspn finely grated lemon rind

2 tblspn plus 125g (4oz) sugar

1 tblspn lemon juice

185g (6oz) self-raising flour

1/2 tspn ground cinnamon

125g (4oz) butter, cut into small cubes

90g (3oz) rolled oats

3 large cooking apples, peeled, cored and thinly sliced

1 Combine dates, water, lemon rind and 2 tablespoons sugar in a saucepan, bring to simmering and cook for 3 minutes or until dates are very soft. Remove from heat, add lemon juice and beat with a wooden spoon until smooth. Cool.

2 Preheat oven to 180°C (350°F/ Gas 4). Sift together flour and cinnamon and rub in butter until mixture resembles coarse bread-crumbs. Add 125g (4oz) sugar and oats and mix well.

3 Press two-thirds of the mixture into a greased and lined 20cm (8in) pie dish or square cake tin. Spread with date mixture and top with apple slices. Sprinkle with remaining crumbs and press firmly. Bake for 45 minutes or until topping is golden.

Serves 6

Strawberry Rhubarb Cobbler

Pineapple Walnut Pudding

90g (3oz) butter

100g (3½oz) caster sugar

1 tspn vanilla essence

2 eggs

4 tblspn milk

125g (4oz) self-raising flour

pinch salt

Caramel Topping

75g (2½oz) butter

170g (5½oz) brown sugar

3-4 slices canned pineapple

6-8 walnut halves

1 To make topping, beat butter and sugar until creamy and spread over bottom and sides of a greased 1 litre (1¾pt) pudding basin. Cut pineapple slices horizontally in half to make 6-8 circles and arrange in bottom and around sides of basin. Place walnuts in centres of rings.

2 Beat butter, sugar and vanilla essence until light and creamy. Beat in eggs, one at a time, then fold in milk, alternately, with sifted flour and salt.

3 Spoon mixture into basin, cover with a double thickness of pleated greaseproof paper and steam for 1½ hours. Serve with fresh cream or custard sauce.

Serves 6

Pears in Red Wine

6 small firm-ripe pears

125g (4oz) sugar

250ml (8fl oz) red wine

125ml (4fl oz) water

strip of lemon rind

1 cinnamon stick

1 Preheat oven to 180°C (350°F/ Gas 4). Peel pears, leaving stems attached. Dissolve sugar in wine and water in a saucepan. Add lemon rind and cinnamon, bring to the boil and boil for 1 minute.

2 Arrange pears upright in an ovenproof dish and pour over wine syrup. Cover and bake for 1 hour or until pears are tender. Cool completely in syrup then chill until cold.

3 Arrange pears in a serving dish, pour syrup over and serve with whipped cream if liked.

Serves 6

Kitchen Tip

If pears are very hard, it may take up to 2 hours baking to tenderise them. If almost ripe, they may be cooked over low heat on top of the stove in prepared wine syrup. Remove pears with a slotted spoon when tender, reduce syrup over high heat and pour over pears.

Lemon Rice Pudding

100g (3½oz) short-grain rice

750ml (1¼pt) milk

1 vanilla bean or 2 tspn vanilla essence

250g (8oz) sugar

125ml (4fl oz) double cream, whipped, optional

2 lemons

1 Wash rice well and cook in boiling water for 2 minutes to remove starch. Drain.

2 Bring milk to the boil, add rice and vanilla bean, if using, and gently simmer for 20 minutes. Add 125g (4oz) sugar and vanilla essence, if using, and stir until sugar dissolves. Turn mixture into serving dish. If using cream, allow rice to cool to room temperature then fold in cream.

3 Cut lemons into thin slices and blanch in boiling water for 3 minutes. Drain. Combine remaining 125g (4oz) sugar and 2 tablespoons water in a small heavy saucepan or frying pan, bring slowly to the boil, add lemon slices and poach for 10-15 minutes or until lemon slices are tender and glazed. Place slices on rice and serve hot or cold.

Serves 4

Banana Bread Pudding

3 large eggs

750ml (1¼pt) milk

250g (8oz) sugar

2 tspn ground cinnamon

1 tspn freshly grated nutmeg

2 tspn vanilla essence

14 slices day-old bread, cubed

90g (3oz) raisins

2 ripe bananas, mashed

125g (4oz) butter

Hot Whisky Sauce

155g (5oz) butter

185g (6oz) sugar

90ml (3fl oz) whisky

2 small eggs, lightly beaten

1 Preheat oven to 160°C (325°F/Gas 3). Whisk together eggs, milk, sugar, half the spices and the vanilla essence. Add bread cubes, raisins and bananas and mix to combine.

2 Pour mixture into a generously greased 32 x 23 x 5cm (12¾ x 9 x 2in) ovenproof dish. Dot with butter, sprinkle with a little extra sugar and remaining spices and bake for 1¼ hours or until set and golden.

3 To make sauce, melt butter in a small, heavy saucepan, add sugar and cook for 2 minutes or until bubbly. Remove from heat and stir in whisky. Return to heat and cook until sugar dissolves.

4 Stir a few spoonfuls of syrup into beaten eggs then return egg mixture to saucepan. Stir over low heat for 10-20 seconds or until sauce is thick. Serve immediately over warm pudding.

Serves 6-8

Lemon Rice Pudding, Pears in Red Wine, Pineapple Walnut Pudding

FRESH AND FRUITY

Fruits, with their variety of colours, perfumes, flavours and textures are perfect dessert partners. This selection spans the season's harvests with new and favourite combinations.

Cherries Jubilee

125g (4oz) sugar

pinch salt

1 tblspn cornflour

250ml (8fl oz) water

500g (1lb) stemmed black cherries, stoned if preferred

2-4 tblspn brandy

1 litre (1³/₄pt) vanilla ice cream

Combine sugar, salt, cornflour and water in a saucepan, add cherries and cook until thickened and bubbly, stirring constantly. Warm the brandy, ignite and pour over the cherries. Spoon cherries immediately over ice cream and serve.

Serves 6

Plum and Port Sauce

Serve over ice cream or ice cream and poached stone fruits such as peaches and nectarines. To poach fruits, refer to recipe for Fruit Compote on page 28.

125g (4oz) sugar

125ml (4fl oz) water

500g (1lb) plums, stoned and cut into eighths

2 tspn finely grated orange rind

2 tblspn tawny port

1 tspn fresh lemon juice, or to taste

pinch cinnamon

pinch salt

1 Dissolve sugar in water in a large saucepan, bring to the boil, stirring, reduce heat and simmer for 5 minutes. Add plums and orange rind and simmer for 10 minutes or until plums are soft, adding more water if necessary.

2 Purée mixture in a blender or food processor then push purée through a fine sieve into a bowl. Stir in port, lemon juice, cinnamon and salt. Cool, cover and chill until cold.

Serves 4

Ricotta with Fruits in Season

This dish depends on perfect fruit and presentation.

125-250g (4-8oz) ricotta cheese

Choose two or three of the following:
1 thick slice of pawpaw, 1 small sliced banana, 8 grapes, 6 strawberries, 1 peeled and sliced kiwi fruit, 60g (2oz) fresh raspberries, 1 peeled and sliced peach, 2 halved and stoned apricots or plums, or 1 halved tamarillo

Fruit Sauce

1 persimmon, fresh strawberries, sieved or passionfruit pulp

Choose a pretty plate and pile ricotta cheese to one side. Arrange prepared fruit choices on plate with ricotta cheese and spoon over sieved persimmon, strawberries or passionfruit pulp. A squeeze of lime juice is a lovely addition.

Serves 1

Cherries Jubilee, Plum and Port Sauce shown with poached peaches and ice cream

Fruit Compote

3 large ripe peaches

6 ripe apricots

6 ripe plums

185g (6oz) sugar

375ml (12fl oz) water

1 tspn vanilla essence or 1 vanilla pod

2 tblspn rum or peach brandy, optional

1 Drop fruits, a few at a time, into boiling water and leave for 1 minute, slip off skins and discard. If liked, halve and remove the stones.

2 Bring sugar, water and vanilla to the boil, add fruits and poach gently for 8-10 minutes or until barely tender. Remove fruits as they cook and place in a bowl.

3 Boil syrup until reduced and thick, cool slightly and pour over fruit. Cool, cover and chill. Add rum or brandy, if using, and serve.

Serves 6

Tart Tatin

You will need a heavy-based, round flame-proof dish such as a cast-iron frying pan with a screw-on handle, or a small paella pan.

10 large ripe Golden Delicious apples

125g (4oz) butter

375g (12oz) sugar

125g (4oz) sugar, extra

squeeze lemon juice

Shortcrust Pastry

125g (4oz) plain flour, sifted

1/2 tblspn caster sugar

90g (3oz) butter, diced

1 egg yolk

1 tblspn cold water

1 To make pastry, combine flour and sugar in a bowl, make a well in the centre, add butter, egg yolk and cold water and mix to make a dough. Chill for 1 hour.

2 Roll out pastry on a lightly floured surface 3mm (1/8in) thick and cut into a 27cm (11in) round. Transfer to a paper-lined tray and chill. Peel and core apples and cut into halves or quarters.

3 Stir butter and sugar in a 23cm (9in) round flameproof dish over low heat until melted. Arrange apples in dish, cut-side-up and close together, in circles. Cook for 12-15 minutes or until a pale caramel forms. Cover apples with pastry, pushing edges inside the dish.

4 Place dish on a baking sheet and bake in a preheated 190°C (375°F/Gas 5) oven for 45 minutes. Cool for 10 minutes. Invert onto a warm serving dish. Caramelise extra sugar in a small, heavy saucepan over low heat adding a few drops lemon juice and drizzle over tart. Serve warm.

Serves 8

Fruit Compote

Bananas with Passionfruit

Oranges, Dates and Pine Nuts

4 Navel oranges

125g (4oz) pitted dates, finely chopped

2 tblspn rum or 2 tspn orange-flower water

3 tblspn pine nuts, toasted

Peel oranges carefully, removing all white pith. Cut into medium slices and arrange in a glass serving bowl. Sprinkle with dates and rum or orange-flower water. Cover tightly and macerate for at least 1 hour. To serve, sprinkle with pinenuts.

Serves 4

Bananas with Passionfruit

4 firm-ripe bananas

45g (1¹/₂oz) brown sugar

60ml (2fl oz) dark rum or orange juice

1 tspn ground ginger

pinch salt

60ml (2fl oz) water

2 tblspn sugar

pulp of 6 passionfruit

45g (1¹/₂oz) butter

1 Peel and cut bananas lengthwise in half. Combine brown sugar, half the rum (or all the orange juice), ginger and salt in a shallow dish, mix well and add bananas, turning to coat.

2 Combine water and sugar in a small saucepan over a medium heat and stir until sugar dissolves and a light syrup forms. Remove from heat, stir in passionfruit pulp and set aside to keep warm.

3 Melt half the butter in a sauté pan or chafing dish over a low heat. Add bananas, cut-side-down, and the sugar mixture and cook for 5 minutes. Add remaining rum, heat until fumes appear and ignite. Shake pan until flames subside and stir in remaining butter.

4 Arrange bananas on serving plates, pour over pan juices, then passionfruit sauce and serve immediately.

Serves 4

Italian Baked Peaches

Italian Baked Peaches

2 tblspn sugar

1 egg yolk

30g (1oz) butter, cut into small pieces

90g (3oz) crushed crisp almond macaroons

4-6 large firm-ripe peaches, halved and stoned

white wine or water

Preheat oven to 180°C (350°F/ Gas 4). Combine sugar, egg yolk, butter and macaroons. Scoop out a little pulp from each peach half, chop finely and mix with biscuit mixture. Pack mixture into peach halves and arrange in a buttered, shallow ovenproof dish. Pour in enough wine or water to cover base of dish and bake for 30 minutes or until tender. Serve hot with cream.

Serves 4-6

Raspberry Syllabub

250g (8oz) fresh raspberries

1 tblspn rose water

60g (2oz) caster sugar

375ml (12fl oz) double cream

125ml (4fl oz) sweet white wine

1 egg white, stiffly beaten

1 Lightly crush half the raspberries, sprinkle with rose water and half the sugar.

2 Beat cream stiffly then gradually add remaining sugar and wine, beating constantly until mixture stands in soft peaks. Add two large spoonfuls of cream to crushed berries and mix well.

3 Lightly fold raspberry mixture, then beaten egg white into remaining cream so that the cream is streaked pale pink. Fold in whole raspberries, reserving a few for the top.

4 Turn mixture into a glass serving bowl, top with reserved berries and chill thoroughly. Serve with dessert biscuits.

Serves 4-6

Strawberries Ena

1 orange

375g (12oz) ripe strawberries, hulled

1 tblspn caster sugar

2 tblspn orange-flavoured liqueur or brandy, optional

185ml (6fl oz) double cream

2 bananas, well mashed

1 tspn brown sugar

4 crisp dessert biscuits

1 Cut a few strips of rind from orange and cut into fine shreds. Peel orange and cut into segments. Combine orange shreds, segments and strawberries (halved if large), sprinkle with caster sugar and liqueur, and chill for 2-3 hours.

2 To serve, pile fruit mixture onto four dessert plates. Beat cream to stiff peaks, fold in bananas and brown sugar and spoon over fruit. Serve with biscuits.

Serves 4-6

Turkish Walnut Tart

155g (5oz) finely chopped walnuts or pecans

45g (1¹/₂oz) dried breadcrumbs

315g (10oz) orange marmalade

2 tblspn orange-flavoured liqueur

100g (3¹/₂oz) unsalted butter, melted and cooled

10 sheets filo pastry

1 tblspn icing sugar

300g (9¹/₂oz) canned mandarin segments, drained

1 Preheat oven to 190°C (375°F/ Gas 5). Combine nuts and breadcrumbs. Stir together 235g (7¹/₂oz) of the marmalade, the liqueur and 2 tablespoons melted butter in a small saucepan over a low heat until warm and combined. Trim filo sheets to 34cm (14in) squares and cover with a barely damp tea-towel.

2 To assemble tart, brush a 20cm (8in) pie plate or round cake tin with melted butter and line with 1 sheet of filo, pressing it flat against sides and bottom with a brush dipped in melted butter. Allow pastry edges to extend over sides, but do not butter the edges.

3 Layer 3 more sheets of filo, brushing each lightly with butter in the same manner. Sprinkle one-third of the nut mixture over pastry, drizzle with

one-third of the marmalade mixture and add 2 more sheets of filo, brushing each with butter. Repeat procedure twice, using remaining pastry, and nut and marmalade mixtures. Brush top of tart with remaining butter.

4 Bake on bottom shelf of oven for 30-35 minutes or until filo is golden brown. If edges brown too quickly, loosely cover with foil.

5 Cool tart on a wire rack for 10 minutes. Heat and strain remaining marmalade. Carefully turn out tart, remove pie plate and quickly turn tart upright onto a serving plate. Sift icing sugar over pastry edges, arrange mandarins in concentric circles in centre and brush with marmalade to glaze. Serve warm.

Serves 6-8

Strawberries Ena

31

Blueberry Buttermilk Tart

125g (4oz) plain flour

pinch salt

60g (2oz) unsalted butter, chopped

2 tblspn caster sugar

2 egg yolks

2 drops vanilla essence

Buttermilk Filling

250ml (8fl oz) buttermilk

3 large egg yolks

125g (4oz) sugar

1 tblspn finely grated lemon rind

1 tblspn lemon juice

60g (2oz) butter, melted and cooled

1 tspn vanilla essence

250-500g (8oz-1lb) blueberries

1 Sift together flour and salt. Make a well in the centre, add butter, sugar, egg yolks and vanilla essence and using fingertips, lightly work mixture into a dough. Gently knead dough, wrap and chill for at least 1 hour.

2 Preheat oven to 190°C (350°F/ Gas 5). Roll out dough on a lightly floured surface to line a 23cm (9in) flan tin with removable base. Chill for 15 minutes. Prick pastry with a fork, line with grease-proof paper, fill with uncooked rice and bake for 20 minutes. Remove paper and rice and bake for 10 minutes longer or until cooked and golden. Cool.

3 Reduce oven to 180°C (350°F/ Gas 4). To make filling, place buttermilk, egg yolks, sugar, lemon rind, lemon juice, butter and vanilla essence in a blender or food processor and blend until smooth. Scatter blueberries in pastry case, pour filling over blueberries and bake for 40 minutes or until filling is just set. Serve chilled or at room temperature.

Serves 6-8

Macédoine of Fruit

60g (2oz) sugar

125ml (4fl oz) water

125ml (4fl oz) sweet or dry vermouth

1 piece cinnamon stick

1 pineapple, peeled and cut into wedges

3 navel oranges, peeled and segmented

1 large bunch grapes, seeded

1 Combine sugar, water, vermouth and cinnamon in a saucepan, bring to the boil, stirring to dissolve sugar. Remove from heat, cover and cool to room temperature.

2 Pour sugar syrup over combined fruit, cover and refrigerate for at least 1 hour to macerate before serving.

Serves 6

Blueberry Buttermilk Tart

Pineapple Custard Tart

Pineapple Custard Tart

75g (2¹/₂oz) caster sugar

2-3 tblspn cornflour

2 egg yolks

2 eggs

500ml (16fl oz) milk, scalded

220g (7oz) canned crushed pineapple, drained

220g (7oz) pineapple rings, drained, syrup reserved

155g (5oz) apricot jam

Sweet Pastry

155g (5oz) plain flour

pinch of salt

75g (2¹/₂oz) unsalted butter, chopped

60g (2oz) caster sugar

1 egg yolk

2 drops vanilla essence

1 To make pastry, sift together flour and salt. Make a well in the centre, add butter, sugar, egg yolk and vanilla essence and using fingertips, lightly work mixture into a dough. Gently knead dough until smooth, wrap and chill for at least 1 hour.

2 Preheat oven to 190°C (375°F/Gas 5). Roll out dough on a lightly floured surface to line a 25cm (10in) flan tin with removable base. Chill for 15 minutes. Prick pastry with a fork, line with greaseproof paper, fill with uncooked rice and bake for 15 minutes. Remove paper and rice and bake for 10 minutes longer or until cooked and golden. Cool.

3 Beat together sugar, cornflour and 2 egg yolks until smooth. Add 2 eggs and beat until combined. Pour hot milk over egg mixture, mix well and transfer to saucepan. Cook over a low heat for 2 minutes, stirring constantly, until thick. Strain custard into a bowl set in a pan of ice and cool completely, stirring. Stir in crushed pineapple, cover and chill thoroughly.

4 Pour custard into pastry case. Arrange pineapple rings over top in overlapping concentric circles. Heat jam with a little reserved pineapple syrup, brush over top to glaze and allow to set before serving.

Serves 8-10

German Apple Dessert Cake

60g (2oz) butter

90g (3oz) sugar

1 egg

125g (4oz) self-raising flour, sifted

60ml (2fl oz) milk

3 medium apples, peeled, quartered and cored

2 tblspn demerara or caster sugar mixed with 1/4 tspn ground cinnamon

whipped sweetened double cream to serve

1 Preheat oven to 180°C (350°F/ Gas 4). Beat butter and sugar until creamy, add egg and beat well. Add half the flour and beat to combine. Stir in milk, alternately, with remaining flour to make a thick batter.

2 Spread batter in a greased 23cm (9in) springform tin. Cut apple quarters into thin slices not quite all the way through and place, cored side down, over batter.

3 Bake for 1 hour or until cake is cooked when tested with a skewer. While still warm sprinkle with cinnamon-sugar mixture. Serve with cream.

Serves 6-8

Pears in Vermouth

500ml (16fl oz) sweet red vermouth

250g (8oz) sugar

125ml (4fl oz) orange juice

1 tspn finely grated orange rind

6-8 firm-ripe pears, peeled, halved and cored

1 lemon, halved

1 Combine vermouth, sugar, orange juice and orange rind in a saucepan. Bring to the boil, stirring to dissolve sugar, and simmer gently for 5 minutes.

2 Rub pears with lemon to prevent browning. Add pears to syrup and simmer for 8-10 minutes or until tender. Cool pears in syrup, then remove to a serving bowl. Boil syrup until reduced to 250ml (8fl oz) and pour over pears. Cool and chill. Serve with sweetened whipped cream flavoured with orange liqueur, if liked.

Serves 6-8

Plum Clafoutis

60g (2oz) butter

750g (1 1/2lb) small ripe plums, halved and stoned

100g (3 1/2oz) caster sugar

2 eggs

6 tblspn plain flour

1/2 tspn vanilla essence

375ml (12fl oz) milk

1 Preheat oven to 200°C (400°F/ Gas 6). Use half the butter to grease a shallow ovenproof dish. Arrange plums in dish and sprinkle with 60g (2oz) of the sugar.

2 Beat eggs lightly. Melt remaining butter, stir in remaining sugar, flour and vanilla essence, add to eggs and beat well to combine. Add enough milk to mixture to make a thick batter.

3 Pour batter over plums and bake for 30 minutes. Reduce oven to 160°C (325°F/Gas 3) and bake for 10 minutes longer or until puffy and crisp at the edges. Sprinkle with a little extra sugar and serve while still hot.

Serves 6

Cherries Wakefield

500g (1lb) cherries, pitted

12 coconut macaroons

4 tblspn fresh orange juice

2 tspn finely grated orange rind

2 tblspn orange-flavoured liqueur

1 tblspn caster sugar

125ml (4fl oz) double cream

1 Place cherries in a glass serving bowl with macaroons broken into 3-4 pieces and half the orange juice and set aside.

2 Combine remaining orange juice, orange rind, liqueur and sugar and stir until sugar dissolves. Beat cream until stiff, gradually adding orange syrup and pile over cherries. Chill for 1 hour before serving.

Serves 4

Normandy Apples

125g (4oz) sugar

310ml (10fl oz) water

6 eating apples, peeled and quartered

3 tblspn apple brandy

Caramel Crack

90g (3oz) sugar

3 tblspn water

1 Place sugar and water in a large saucepan and heat gently, stirring until sugar dissolves. Bring to the boil, reduce heat and simmer for 5 minutes.

2 Add apples to syrup, cover and gently poach for 15-20 minutes or until apples are transparent. Remove from heat and set aside to cool in the syrup.

3 Using a slotted spoon, transfer apples to a serving dish. Boil syrup rapidly until reduced by half, stir in brandy and pour over apples. Set aside to cool.

4 To make caramel, place sugar and water in a saucepan and heat gently, stirring, until sugar dissolves. Bring to the boil and boil until syrup is golden. Pour onto an oiled baking sheet and set aside to harden. When set, crack into pieces and sprinkle over apples. Serve with dessert biscuits, if liked.

Serves 6

Pears in Vermouth, German Apple Dessert Cake

Rice Tyrolhof

100g (3¹/₂oz) short-grain rice

750ml (1¹/₄pt) milk

2 tblspn sugar

2 tspn gelatine dissolved in 4 tblspn
fresh orange juice

1 apple, cored and diced

125g (4oz) grapes, seeded

90g (3oz) strawberries, sliced

3 tspn rum

125ml (4fl oz) double cream, whipped

whipped cream, to serve

Apricot Sauce

220g (7oz) canned apricot halves

60g (2oz) sugar

2 tspn cornflour blended with
60ml (2fl oz) sherry

2 tspn finely grated lemon rind

1 Place rice and milk in a heavy saucepan, cover and cook over low heat until rice is tender. Add sugar and dissolved gelatine mixture, mix well and set aside to cool completely, stirring occasionally. Fold in prepared fruit, rum and whipped cream. Spoon into a serving dish and chill thoroughly. Just prior to serving, spread extra whipped cream over rice.

2 To make sauce, drain apricots, reserving 125ml (4fl oz) syrup. Purée apricots and place in a small saucepan with reserved syrup, sugar and cornflour mixture. Bring to the boil, stirring until sauce is thick. Remove from heat, stir in lemon rind and serve hot or cold over rice.

Serves 6

Passionfruit Blueberry Cream

300g (9¹/₂oz) fresh or frozen thawed
blueberries

sugar, to taste

1 tspn cornflour blended with 1 tblspn
cold water

8 passionfruit

2 tspn gelatine

125g (4oz) sugar

185ml (6fl oz) double cream

2 egg whites

extra blueberries for garnish

1 Purée berries and rub through a sieve into saucepan. Add sugar and cornflour mixture and bring to simmering. Simmer for 1 minute. Cool, cover and chill.

Rice Tyrolhof

Passionfruit Blueberry Cream

2 Scrape passionfruit pulp and juice from seeds through a sieve into a small bowl. Discard seeds. In a small saucepan, soften gelatine in 90ml (3fl oz) water and heat gently, stirring until dissolved. Add another 90ml (3fl oz) water and the sugar and heat without boiling, stirring until sugar dissolves. Pour into a bowl and stir in passionfruit. Chill until mixture sets to the consistency of raw egg whites.

3 Beat cream until stiff and fold in passionfruit mixture. With clean beaters, beat egg whites until stiff peaks form and fold into mixture. Spoon into dessert glasses, alternately, with blueberry mixture to form layers. Chill until set. Garnish with extra blueberries.

Serves 4

Blueberry Peach Pie

8 ripe peaches, peeled, stoned and sliced

300g (9¹/₂oz) blueberries

250g (8oz) sugar

3 tblspn quick-cooking tapioca

1¹/₂ tspn finely grated lemon rind

¹/₂ tspn ground cinnamon

2 tblspn fresh lemon juice

2 tblspn butter, cut into pieces

1 egg beaten with 1 tspn water and pinch salt to glaze

Sweet Pastry

125g (4oz) plain flour

1 tblspn sugar

90g (3oz) butter

1 egg

1 tblspn iced water

1 To make pastry, combine flour and sugar and rub in butter with fingertips until mixture resembles fine breadcrumbs. Add egg and iced water and mix to make a firm dough. Knead gently, wrap and chill for 1 hour.

2 Preheat oven to 190°C (375°F/ Gas 5). Toss together peaches, blueberries, sugar, tapioca, lemon rind, cinnamon, lemon juice and butter and place in a buttered 2 litre (3¹/₂pt) round ovenproof dish.

3 Roll out dough to fit over dish, crimping the edge decoratively. Brush pastry with egg mixture to glaze, cut vents for steam and bake pie for 1 hour or until filling is bubbling and pastry golden. Serve warm.

Serves 6-8

ELEGANT ENTERTAINERS

What better occasion for dessert than an elegant celebration at home. Look no further for a stylish and original finish for your next dinner party menu.

Vanilla Bavarian Cream

4 egg yolks

170g (5¹/₂oz) caster sugar

pinch salt

375ml (12fl oz) milk, scalded

1 tblspn gelatine, softened in 60ml (2fl oz) water

2 tspn vanilla essence

375ml (12fl oz) double cream, stiffly beaten

raspberries or other fruit, grated chocolate, toasted almonds to decorate

Raspberry Sauce

250g (8oz) fresh or frozen thawed raspberries

125g (4oz) sugar

1-2 tblspn fresh lemon juice

1 Beat egg yolks, sugar and salt in top of a double saucepan until very thick and pale. Stir in warm milk, place over simmering water and cook, stirring, until mixture coats the spoon. Stir in gelatine mixture until dissolved. Remove from heat, stir in vanilla essence, cool, then chill until mixture begins to set.

2 Fold cream into mixture and pour into a 1.5 litre (2¹/₂pt) mould, or six individual moulds, rinsed in cold water. Chill until set.

3 To make sauce, gently heat berries, sugar and lemon juice to taste, lightly mashing the fruit. Purée in a blender then push through a sieve. Cool, then chill.

4 To serve, unmould dessert onto a chilled serving plate. Decorate with fruit, chocolate or almonds and serve with sauce.

Serves 6

Rolled Berry Pavlova

4 egg whites

pinch salt

140g (4¹/₂oz) caster sugar

1 tspn cornflour

1 tspn vinegar

¹/₂ tspn vanilla essence

extra caster sugar, for rolling

300ml (9¹/₂fl oz) double cream

pulp of 6 passionfruit

Berry Coulis

185g (6oz) strawberries or raspberries

1 tblspn icing sugar

squeeze of lemon juice

1 Preheat oven to 180°C (350°F/ Gas 4). Line a 26 x 32cm (10¹/₂ x 12³/₄in) Swiss roll tin with baking paper and lightly oil.

2 Beat egg whites and salt to stiff peaks. Gradually beat in 100g (3¹/₂oz) sugar, then fold in remaining sugar, cornflour, vinegar and vanilla essence. Spread evenly into tin and bake for 12-15 minutes or until just set.

3 Turn onto a clean tea-towel sprinkled with extra sugar. Carefully remove paper and cool for 5 minutes. Using tea-towel, roll up from the long end. Cool for 30 minutes.

4 Beat cream to soft peaks and fold in passionfruit pulp. Unroll pavlova and spread with filling. Re-roll up and chill for 20-30 minutes.

5 To make coulis, crush berries and push through a sieve. Add icing sugar and lemon juice.

Serves 8

Vanilla Bavarian Cream, Rolled Berry Pavlova, Vanilla Custard Pots (page 21)

Chocolate Mousse with Crème Anglaise

4 large egg yolks

60g (2oz) caster sugar

1 tblspn brandy

185g (6oz) dark chocolate, broken into pieces

1¹/₂ tblspn extra strong black coffee

60g (2oz) butter, cubed

125ml (4fl oz) double cream

blanched julienne strips of orange rind for garnish

Orange Crème Anglaise

315ml (10fl oz) milk (or half double cream, half milk)

3 egg yolks

2 tblspn caster sugar

1 tspn cornflour or arrowroot

1 tspn finely grated orange rind

1 Beat egg yolks with caster sugar in a heatproof bowl set over a saucepan of simmering water for 5 minutes or until thick and fluffy. Add brandy and continue beating until mixture triples in volume and holds soft peaks. Remove bowl from heat, place in a bowl of crushed ice and beat until mixture is cool.

2 Melt chocolate with coffee, stirring until smooth, then beat in butter pieces until melted and combined. Fold chocolate mixture into egg mixture then fold in cream. Cover and chill until firm, at least several hours or overnight.

3 To make crème anglaise, scald milk in a heavy saucepan over low heat. Beat egg yolks, caster sugar and cornflour or arrowroot in a bowl until thick and light, pour in hot milk add orange rind and mix well. Transfer mixture to clean saucepan and cook over a very low heat, stirring constantly, until custard thickens and coats the spoon. Pour custard into a jug and set aside to cool, stirring occasionally. Chill.

4 To serve, use a heated serving spoon to scoop egg-shaped portions of mousse onto dessert plates. Pour a little crème anglaise around each and scatter with strips of orange rind.

Serves 8

Chocolate Hazelnut Pavlova

4 egg whites

pinch salt

315g (10oz) caster sugar

1¹/₂ tspn vinegar

1¹/₂ tspn vanilla essence

100g (3¹/₂oz) ground hazelnuts

300ml (9¹/₂fl oz) double cream, whipped

Chocolate Mousse with Crème Anglaise

Hot Passionfruit Soufflé

3 tblspn chopped toasted hazelnuts

Rich Chocolate Sauce

100g (3½oz) dark chocolate, roughly chopped

60g (2oz) caster sugar

1 tspn cocoa powder

185ml (6fl oz) water

vanilla essence to taste

1 Lightly oil and flour a 23cm (9in) springform tin. Preheat oven to150°C (300°F/Gas 2).

2 Beat egg whites with salt to stiff peaks. Gradually add caster sugar, 1 tablespoon at a time, beating constantly. Fold in vinegar, vanilla essence and hazelnuts.

3 Spoon mixture into prepared tin and bake for 1 hour. Turn off heat and cool in oven. (If using a gas range bake at 150°C (300°F/Gas 2) for 1 hour, then turn heat to 120°C (250°F/Gas ½) and bake for 30 minutes longer before turning off heat.)

4 To make sauce, place chocolate in a saucepan with sugar, cocoa and half the water. Bring to the boil over a moderate heat, stirring to dissolve chocolate. Reduce heat and simmer for 2-3 minutes. Add remaining water and vanilla essence, bring to the boil, reduce heat and simmer for 15-20 minutes or until syrupy. Cool.

5 Remove pavlova from tin. It will collapse slightly. Decorate with whipped cream, spoon over some of the sauce and sprinkle with chopped hazelnuts. Serve remaining sauce separately.

Serves 8

Hot Passionfruit Soufflés

butter and caster sugar for soufflé cups

pulp of 6 large passionfruit

100g (3½oz) caster sugar

60ml (2fl oz) water

4 egg whites

1 Preheat oven to 190°C (375°F/ Gas 5). Butter six individual soufflé dishes and dust insides with caster sugar. Scoop passionfruit pulp into a blender or food processor, process for a few seconds only, then strain seeds from juice, reserving 1 tablespoon seeds.

2 Combine 100g (3½oz) caster sugar and water in a saucepan, bring to the boil and boil until syrup reaches soft ball stage.

3 Beat egg whites until stiff then gradually pour in syrup in a thin stream, beating constantly until meringue stands in soft peaks. Fold in passionfruit juice and reserved seeds. Spoon into prepared dishes and level the tops.

4 Place dishes on a baking sheet and bake for 12-15 minutes or until golden and risen. Serve immediately.

Serves 6

White Chocolate Mousse

200g (6½oz) white chocolate, roughly chopped

2 tblspn double cream

60g (2oz) butter, cut into pieces

3 large eggs, separated

60g (2oz) dark chocolate

1 Melt white chocolate with cream in a heatproof bowl over hot water. Remove from heat and add butter, beating briskly until cooled and creamy. Beat in egg yolks, one at a time, until combined. Beat egg whites to soft peaks and fold into mixture. Pour into individual mousse pots or glasses and chill for several hours or overnight.

2 Melt dark chocolate and pour into a piping bag fitted with a fine piping tube. Decorate tops of mousses with swirls of dark chocolate and return to refrigerator to set. The chocolate will become hard and must be broken to get to the creamy mousse underneath.

Serves 6

Hot Chocolate Soufflés

125g (4oz) dark chocolate

3 tblspn brandy or black coffee

5 eggs, separated

4 tblspn sugar

250ml (8fl oz) double cream, whipped, to serve

1 Preheat oven to 190°C (375°F/Gas 5). Melt chocolate with brandy or coffee in a heatproof bowl over hot water. Beat egg yolks with sugar until very pale and thick. Beat in chocolate mixture. Beat egg whites until firm but not dry and fold in chocolate mixture.

2 Spoon mixture into four 185ml (6fl oz) or six 125ml (4fl oz) capacity greased individual soufflé dishes, filling three-quarters full.

3 Place dishes well apart on a baking sheet. Bake on bottom shelf of oven for 15-18 minutes or until risen and brown. Serve immediately on heated plates with whipped cream – each guest makes a hole in the centre of the soufflé and fills it with a spoonful of cream.

Serves 4-6

White Chocolate Mousse

Meringues (on tray) as swirls sandwiched with cream and as fingers dipped in chocolate and nuts, egg-shaped meringues (on plate) served with cream and berry coulis

Meringues

3 large egg whites

1/8 tspn cream of tartar

220g (7oz) caster sugar

sweetened whipped cream to serve

1 Preheat oven to 120°C (250°F/ Gas 1/2). Brush baking sheets lightly with oil and dust with flour or line sheets with baking paper.

2 Beat egg whites until frothy. Add cream of tartar and continue beating until soft peaks form. Gradually add 2 tablespoons of the sugar and beat for 2-3 minutes. Add remaining sugar all at once and quickly fold in using a large metal spoon.

3 Spoon or pipe meringue mixture into desired shapes on prepared sheets as directed. Bake for 1 1/2 hours. Ease meringues from sheets, turn over and return to oven for a further 30 minutes or until crisp, dry and a delicate beige in colour. When cool store in airtight containers. Sandwich meringues with whipped cream and garnish as desired.

Serves 6-8

Variations

To shape meringues with spoons: Take a spoonful of the meringue mixture in a wet dessertspoon and with a wet spatula, quickly smooth it over, piling it in the centre and pointing the two ends. With a second spoon, scoop meringue out onto prepared baking sheet, leaving a 2cm (3/4in) space between each meringue. Bake meringues until crisp, remove from the oven, make a hollow indentation in the base of each by pressing gently with a finger and return to oven to dry completely.

To make piped meringues: Spoon meringue into a forcing bag with a plain nozzle and pipe rounds, wider at the base and spiralling to a peak. Bake as directed.

To make meringue fingers: Pipe meringue through a plain nozzle into small finger lengths on prepared baking sheets.

To chocolate coat one end: Have ready a small bowl of melted chocolate and a saucer of finely chopped nuts. Dip either one or both ends of meringue fingers into chocolate, then sprinkle lightly with nuts. Place on a wire rack to set chocolate.

Honeycomb Mould

Honeycomb Mould

3 large eggs, separated

thinly pared rind of 2 lemons

5 tspn gelatine

90g (3oz) sugar

170ml (5¹/₂fl oz) double cream

375ml (12fl oz) milk, scalded

4 tblspn fresh lemon juice

1 Place egg yolks in a large heatproof bowl, add lemon rind, gelatine, sugar and cream. Gradually add hot milk, stirring to combine.

2 Place bowl over simmering water and stir until mixture almost reaches boiling point and thickens to the consistency of thick cream. Add lemon juice to taste. Remove from heat. Beat egg whites until stiff but not dry and fold in lemon mixture using a large metal spoon.

3 Pour mixture into a wetted 1.2 litre (2pt) jelly mould, allow to stand for 30 minutes at room temperature then chill until set.

4 Run a thin metal spatula 1cm (¹/₂in) wide around edge of pudding and unmould.

Serves 6-8

Lemon Soufflé

3 large eggs, separated

170g (5¹/₂oz) caster sugar

3 tspn finely grated lemon rind

4-5 tblspn fresh lemon juice

300ml (9¹/₂fl oz) double cream, whipped

3 tspn gelatine softened in 3 tblspn water

2 tblspn flaked almonds, toasted, to decorate

1 Tie a band of double thickness greaseproof paper around a 15cm (6in) soufflé dish to stand 5cm (2in) above the rim; oil the inside of the paper.

2 Place egg yolks, sugar and lemon rind in a bowl. Heat lemon juice in a small saucepan, pour over egg mixture and beat with electric mixer until thick. Fold in two-thirds of the cream.

3 Stir soaked gelatine in a heatproof bowl over simmering water until dissolved. Add to the soufflé mixture and stir constantly until mixture begins to set. Beat egg whites until stiff peaks form, fold into lemon mixture and pour into prepared dish. Chill until set.

4 Remove paper collar carefully and press the nuts around the sides. Spread some of the remaining cream over top of soufflé and pipe remainder around the edge. Chill until ready to serve.

Serves 6-8

Chocolate Chestnut Cream

2 egg yolks

60g (2oz) caster sugar

315ml (10fl oz) milk, scalded

100g (3¹/₂oz) dark chocolate, melted

2 tspn gelatine

2 tblspn water

410g (13oz) canned unsweetened chestnut purée

2 tblspn brandy

155ml (5fl oz) double cream

extra cream and shaved chocolate or whole chestnuts in syrup (marron glacé) to decorate

1 Beat egg yolks and sugar in a heatproof bowl until pale and thick. Slowly pour in hot milk, stirring constantly. Place over simmering water and stir until thickened. Stir in melted chocolate. Soften gelatine in water and stir over hot water until gelatine dissolves. Stir into custard.

2 Place custard, chestnut purée and brandy into a food processor or blender and process until smooth. Alternatively, beat chestnut purée and brandy into custard. Beat cream stiffly and fold into chestnut mixture.

3 Pour mixture into an oiled 11 x 21cm (4¹/₂ x 8¹/₂in) loaf tin and chill until set.

4 To serve, turn out of tin and cut into thick slices. Top with a swirl of whipped cream and chocolate shavings or two chestnuts with a little syrup.

Serves 6

Mocha Cream Custards

375ml (12fl oz) milk

250ml (8fl oz) double cream

1 tblspn caster sugar

1 tspn instant coffee powder

45g (1¹/₂oz) chocolate, roughly chopped

4 egg yolks

1 egg

1 Place milk, cream, sugar, coffee powder and chocolate in a saucepan and bring to simmering, stirring to melt chocolate. Remove from heat, cover and cool to lukewarm.

2 Preheat oven to 180°C (350°F/ Gas 4). Beat egg yolks with egg in a bowl and slowly pour in cream mixture. Mix well, then strain into a jug. Pour carefully into small soufflé cups or custard pots.

3 Place dishes in a shallow baking tin filled with enough boiling water to come halfway up the sides of dishes. Cover tin with foil and bake for 12-20 minutes or until set.

4 Carefully remove the tin from oven and remove foil carefully so that no water falls into the custards. Remove dishes from water and cool completely.

Serves 8

Chocolate Chestnut Cream

Cigarettes Russes

Cook 3 or 4 biscuits at one time – at first you may like to cook just one – until you have mastered the art of rolling them.

2 egg whites

100g (3¹/₂oz) caster sugar

60g (2oz) unsalted butter, melted and slightly cooled

60g (2oz) plain flour, sifted

¹/₂ tspn vanilla essence

1 Preheat oven to 200°C (400°F/ Gas 6). Place egg whites in a small bowl and break them up with a fork. Add sugar and beat with a fork until smooth. Stir in butter, flour and vanilla essence and mix to make a smooth batter.

2 Spread tablespoons of the mixture into oblong shapes on a well-greased baking sheet and bake for 5 minutes. Cool slightly before sliding off with a metal spatula and rolling quickly around the handle of a wooden spoon (while rolling one leave the others on the baking sheet to keep warm). After about 10 seconds remove the spoon and roll the next biscuit.

3 Cool completely and store in an airtight container. In humid weather these will soften quickly. Serve with ice creams, mousses or fruit desserts or on their own with coffee.

Makes about 24 biscuits

Almond Bread

3 egg whites

100g (3¹/₂oz) caster sugar

125g (4oz) plain flour, sifted

155g (5oz) whole unblanched slivered almonds

1 tspn vanilla essence

1 Preheat oven to 180°C (350°F/ Gas 4). Beat egg whites until stiff but not dry, then gradually beat in sugar until mixture is thick and glossy. Using a metal spoon fold in flour, almonds and vanilla essence, mixing well. Turn mixture into a well-greased or non-stick small loaf tin.

2 Bake for 30 minutes or until pale golden and firm to touch. Allow to cool in tin, then turn out and wrap in foil. Chill overnight. This will help you to cut thin, even slices.

3 Preheat oven to 150°C (300°F/ Gas 2). Cut loaf into thin slices and place on an ungreased baking sheet. Bake until golden. Cool and store in an airtight container. Serve with a fruit or creamy dessert or with coffee.

Makes about 36

Almond Tuiles

90g (3oz) unsalted butter

75g (2¹/₂oz) caster sugar

60g (2oz) plain flour

pinch salt

90g (3oz) slivered almonds

1 Preheat oven to 200°C (400°F/ Gas 6). Beat butter until creamy then beat in sugar until light and fluffy. Sift flour with salt and fold into creamed mixture with almonds.

2 Place teaspoons of mixture on a greased baking sheet, leaving room for spreading, and flatten with a wet fork.

3 Bake for 6 minutes or until golden. Allow to cool a few seconds on sheet, then transfer, using a metal spatula, to the end of a rolling pin and slightly curl. It takes only a few seconds for the biscuits to curve into their characteristic shape.

4 Set finished biscuits aside to cool and store in an airtight container. Serve with fruit desserts.

Makes about 24

Brandy Snaps

60g (2oz) butter

60g (2oz) brown sugar

125g (4oz) golden syrup

60g (2oz) plain flour, sifted

1 tspn ground ginger

1 Preheat oven to 180°C (350°F/ Gas 4). Place butter, sugar and golden syrup in a saucepan and heat gently until butter melts and sugar dissolves. Cool slightly, stir in flour and ginger and beat well.

2 Place teaspoonfuls of mixture 10cm (4in) apart on a baking sheet. Bake for 10-12 minutes or until golden. Cool slightly, then remove with a palette knife and roll around the handle of a wooden spoon, keeping the smooth side of the wafer to the handle of the spoon. Leave for 1-2 minutes to set, then slip off carefully onto a wire rack to cool. Store in an airtight container. Serve plain or filled with whipped cream.

Makes 16

Kitchen Tip

If the mixture cools and becomes too thick, spread it out thinly with a palette knife to flatten. If the biscuits become too brittle to roll, return them to the oven for 30 seconds to soften.

Almond Tuiles, Almond Bread, Cigarettes Russes

Index

Managing Editor: Rachel Blackmore
Editors: Kirsten John, Linda Venturoni
Production Manager: Sheridan Carter
Senior Production Editor: Anna Maguire
Picture Editor: Kirsten Holmes
Production Editor: Sheridan Packer
Editorial and Production Assistant: Danielle Thiris
Layout and Finished Art: Stephen Joseph
Styling Cover and Additional Internal Shots:
Janet Mitchell

Published by J.B. Fairfax Press Pty Limited
80-82 McLachlan Avenue
Rushcutters Bay, NSW 2011
A.C.N. 003 738 430

Formatted by J.B.Fairfax Press Pty Limited
Printed by Toppan Printing Co, Hong Kong
PRINTED IN HONG KONG

JBFP 383 A/UK
Includes Index
ISBN 1 86343 116 0 (set)
ISBN 1 86343 216 7

Distribution and Sales Enquiries
Australia: J.B. Fairfax Press Pty Limited
Ph: (02) 361 6366 Fax: (02) 360 6262
United Kingdom: J.B. Fairfax Press Limited
Ph (01933) 402330 Fax: (01933) 402234